QUEEN
ELIZABETH II
BOTANIC
PARK

One With Nature

THE
DONNING COMPANY
PUBLISHERS

QUEEN • ELIZABETH • II

BOTANIC
PARK
CAYMAN ISLANDS

QUEEN ELIZABETH II BOTANIC PARK

One With Nature

Editing and Production: David Martins

Coauthors: David Martins • Andrew Guthrie

Features: Fred Burton • Frank Roulstone

Principal Photography: Tanja Braendle Slattery • Miguel Escalante • Sean Slattery • Kevin T. Carlson

Additional Photography: Michael Gore • Richard Ground • Fred Burton • David Martins • Andrew Guthrie • John Vlitos • Carol Winker

Cayman Islands Tourism Attractions Board—Grand Cayman—Cayman Islands

TANJA BRAENDLE SLATTERY

The vibrant red flower of the Red Powder Puff (*Calliandra haemato-cephala*).

Queen Elizabeth II Botanic Park
Box 203NS, North Side, Grand Cayman, Cayman Islands.
Telephone: 345–947–9462 • Fax: 345–947–7873
website: http://www.botanic-park.ky

The Donning Company Publishers
184 Business Park Drive, Suite 206
Virginia Beach, VA 23462

Steve Mull, General Manager
Barbara A. Bolton, Project Director
Pam Forrester, Project Researcher
Dawn V. Kofroth, Assistant General Manager
Sally Clarke Davis, Editor
Marshall McClure, Senior Graphic Designer
John Harrell, Imaging Artist
Scott Rule, Director of Marketing

Library of Congress Cataloging-in-Publication Data

Martins, David, 1935–
    Queen Elizabeth II Botanic Park : one with nature / coauthors, David Martins, Andrew Guthrie.
       p. cm.
    ISBN 1-57864-179-9 (hardcover : alk. paper) — ISBN 1-57864-180-2 (pbk : alk. paper)
       1. Queen Elizabeth II Botanic Park (Cayman Islands) I. Guthrie, Andrew, 1960– II. Title

SB484.C29 M37 2002
333.78'3'0972921—dc21

                                                                              2002073650

Printed in the United States of America

The production of this book was funded in part by the generosity of three major donors:

CONTENTS

CAROL WINKER

CAROL WINKER

A view of the entrance pond in the early days of the Botanic Park's development with the Park's first Horticulturist, Jennie Leigh Lane, in the background.

Inset: **Her Majesty Queen Elizabeth II officially opens the Botanic Park on 7 February 1994 while then-Minister for Tourism, Aviation, and Planning, Mr. Thomas Jefferson, applauds.**

"I Come to the Park"

. . . to revel in the power and texture of life in nature

. . . to find relaxation and serenity

. . . to be amazed again at the beauty of God's work

. . . to restore myself.

HOW IT BEGAN

The idea for a Botanic Park in Cayman grew out of the original impetus in the early 1980s to create the National Trust of the Cayman Islands, and after an initially fruitless search the land for the Park was received gratis. A real estate developer's donation of thirty acres of virgin land donated to the Trust and thirty acres to the Government, were combined with five acres of Government land to create the sixty-five-acre facility.

The Park and its Mission

The early work in and development of the Park is a story of scores of volunteers, including prison inmates, putting in countless hours of work, supported by a range of donations, in cash and kind, from

CAROL WINKER

Joyce Hylton and Frank Roulstone along the Woodland Trail attaching the rare endemic Ghost Orchid (*Dendrophylax fawcettii*) to Buttonwood (*Conocarpus erectus*) branches as part of a conservation programme to save this endangered species.

many sectors in the society. In the early going, there was significant dispute about the direction the Park should take with some arguing for a pristine wilderness approach while others were pushing for a decorative garden concept. The Park was formally opened by Queen Elizabeth II and named for her on the occasion of her visit to the Cayman Islands in 1993. Administered initially by the National Trust, the Park was put under the Ministry of Tourism in 1994 and given an annual Government grant. At that stage, the decision was taken to combine the wilderness and decorative approaches in order to make the venture commercially viable. This combination of interests, which was highly praised by horticulturalists, gives the Park a unique place in the panoply of such developments around the world. Now an established fact in the community, the Queen Elizabeth II Botanic Park is achieving its twin aim of preserving large tracts of virgin land while also showcasing an attractive array of nature's decorations.

The mission of the Park was intended to be three-fold:

• **Recreation**—It is a green space that provides enjoyment and is therefore a tourism attraction as well as an entity for Caymanians' benefit.

• **Education**—Making persons aware of plants, animals, conservation, gardening, practical and historical use of plants, etc.

• **Conservation**—The Park area includes a nature preserve section that cannot be interfered with, and it is also the site of conservation projects for some plants found only in Cayman, which we now propagate here. It is also the site of the National Trust's successful iguana breeding programme.

Andrew Guthrie, Botanic Park general manager since 1995.

Volunteer Bonnie McTaggart checks the progress of seedlings in the Nursery mist beds.

Right: Joyce Hylton mists the orchids on exhibit during the very popular annual Orchid Show.

JOHN VLITOS

THE VOLUNTEERS

Apart from the largesse of individual donors, the Park owes its creation to scores of volunteers from all walks of life who have devoted hundreds of hours to the project for the sheer love of the venture.

My involvement with the Botanic Park began in the early days and I have watched its development over the years. I am very proud of the Botanic Park, and throughout my travels in the Caribbean, I have yet to see a botanical garden that matches the quality and beauty of ours.

—Sallie Hislop
(gardening enthusiast)

Above: As part of one of the Park's programmes, Kirkland Nixon lectures on orchid culture.

Top: Frank Roulstone demonstrates how to propagate orchids by seed during the annual Orchid Show.

Right: One of the Park's most dedicated volunteers, Lisa Brodlie prepares to repot palm seedlings in the Nursery.

DAVE MARTINS

The Floral Garden

The design intent of the Floral Garden was to create an informal garden in which one could alternate between floral displays, then wooded areas with native trees, and into open, grassy spaces. It was also laid out by colours, starting with pink and working through seven shades.

The Red Garden

In this section of the garden—wooded, shady, and home to a number of large-

The showy colourful pendant bracts of the inflorescence of *Heliconia rostrata*.

TANJA BRAENDLE SLATTERY

TANJA BRAENDLE SLATTERY

Left: **The vibrant red flowers of the Water Lily (*Nymphaea* cv. 'Red Flare') open every morning and close by noon.**

The colourful leaves of the Croton plant (*Codiaeum variegatum* cv. 'Thomas Edison') show why these plants are popular ornamentals.

MIGUEL ESCALANTE

leafed plants—there is more of a tropical rain forest feeling than anywhere else in the Botanic Park.

HELICONIA

It can easily be mistaken for a Banana plant because the leaves are almost identical, and when in bloom it's also mistaken for a Bird of Paradise (*Strelitzia reginae*), but it is in fact the ubiquitous Heliconia, found in a variety of colours and with some species reaching a height of eighteen to twenty feet. What appears to be flowers on this plant are actually colourful bracts that also hold water and are therefore a favourite spot for young frogs. Heliconias (not native to Cayman) are pollinated by hummingbirds (not found in Cayman) and no seed set occurs here.

MIGUEL ESCALANTE

Though not edible, the fruits of the Australian Carpentaria Palm (*Carpentaria acuminata*) provide months of colour in the Red Garden.

Related to the ginger of culinary fame, Red Ginger (*Alpinia purpurata*) blooms every day of the year.

MIGUEL ESCALANTE

GINGERS

In this garden you will find the Ginger Lily (*Alpinia purpurata*), related to the culinary variety, and featuring brightly-coloured red bracts that look like flowers. Bruising the flowers can produce a faint whiff of ginger. Since the flowers last a long time, the Ginger Lily is in bloom all year round. The garden is also home to the Indonesian Wax Ginger (*Tapeinochilos ananassae*), with its flowers at the base of the plant, as well as the Soap Ginger, so named because squeezing the stalks produces a soapy liquid.

Known locally as Cat Tail (*Acalypha hispida*) this plant produces a rope-like inflorescence with the feel of chenille, thus the more widely known name of Chenille Plant.

MIGUEL ESCALANTE

WATER LILY

The lilies (*Nymphaea*) in this pond combine burgundy leaves with rich red flowers. The flowers are in bloom virtually every day of the year, but if you want to see them, come in the morning; in the afternoon they go to sleep and stay closed.

CROTONS

Native to Southeast Asia, Croton (*Codiaeum variegatum*) is almost a fixture in Caribbean life in yards and at roadsides. Related to Poinsettia (*Euphorbia pulcherrima*), it should be planted where there is adequate space since frequent pruning degrades the shape of the plant. Partial shade, as opposed to direct sunlight, produces the most vivid colours in Croton leaves.

CHENILLE

Known in Cayman as the Cat Tail, the Chenille (*Acalypha hispida*) blooms almost every day of the year and produces long flowers that supposedly feel like the fabric chenille and that also look like, yes, a cat's tail. With each leaf producing a "cat tail," the plant can be a striking sight with as many as two hundred of these hanging flowers on display at one time.

MICHAEL GORE

A commonly seen resident of the Botanic Park is the West Indian Woodpecker (*Melanerpes superciliaris*). This woodpecker has found the fruit of the Christmas Palm (*Veitchia merrillii*) to its liking.

HIBISCUS

The Double Red Hibiscus (*Hibiscus rosa-sinensis*) variety in our Park, also known as the Jamaican Red, l.as been trained to grow with one trunk (two to three feet) and then allowed to branch out, resulting in a tree-like appearance. The flowers are double, which means they have double petals and no reproductive parts. The standard variety is an extremely popular plant, found all over Cayman; it blooms almost every day, but the individual flowers close up at night and live for only twenty-four hours.

BROMELIAD

An unusual feature of this garden is the naturally occurring Wild Fig (*Ficus aurea*) with its aerial roots hanging down in the sinkhole. The terrestrial Bromeliad (*Neoregelia*) can be used, as in this case, to beautify an area with its yellow stripes and red splotches. The plant's rosettes collect water, making it a good place to find small frogs or even water bugs. Unfortunately, it is also a prime breeding location for mosquitoes.

CARPENTERIA

This palm (*Carpentaria acuminata*) produces bright red fruit that are beautiful to look it but are not edible; however, in its native Australia the Aborigines eat the heart of the palm, or cabbage. As is the case with most plants in the Park, the Carpenteria is difficult to grow in environs close to the sea.

ANNATTO

This plant (*Bixa orellana*) produces pink flowers that look like roses that are then followed by red seed pods. The seeds produce a yellow dye that was used by the Carib Indians for ornamental body painting. Commonly sold in spice departments in grocery stores, the seeds are used to create the distinctively flavoured Annatto oil used in cooking.

The Orange Garden

The emphasis in this open part of the Park is on featuring plants that love to be in the sunlight. This is the second largest area in the Floral Garden.

CANARY ISLAND DATE PALM

Very prevalent in the Middle East, this palm (*Phoenix canariensis*) is notable for its orange fruits and its distinctive bulge below the crown. This bulge is the accumulation of the bases of dead leaves still clinging to the trunk. In humid conditions, such as in the Queen Elizabeth II Botanic Park, the palm also becomes host to a number of ferns that enhances the beauty of its orange-coloured but inedible fruit. Care should be taken to avoid the long needle-like thorns at the base of the palm fronds.

FISH TAIL PALM

Individual leaflets in the shape of a fish's tail give the plant (*Caryota no*) its name. Although fast growing, the plant does not bloom until thirty to thirty-five years old. It stays in bloom for about four to five years with flowers in the shape of long rope-like structures. After blooming for several years, the plant dies.

Named Shrimp Plant (*Justicia brandegeana*) due to the resemblance of its colourful inflorescence to the popular crustacean, this herbaceous plant provides year-round colour in the Orange Garden.

TANJA BRAENDLE SLATTERY

15

TANJA BRAENDLE SLATTERY

One of the most frequently encountered birds by visitors to the Botanic Park is the Bananaquit (*Coereba flaveola*) that can be seen here feeding from the inflorescence of the Shrimp Plant (*Justicia brandegeana*).

AECHMEA BLANCHETIANA

Probably the most striking feature of the Orange Garden is this bromeliad, planted in a mass, with its completely orange leaves. The bloom, a long stalk, is also orange. Because of its overall orange colour, and the absence of green foliage, visitors often assume the plant is ailing.

COSTUS

Like the Heliconia, this plant produces long stalks at the end of which is a cone-shaped formation of bracts. The individual flowers, coming out of those bracts, are orange in colour. Because of its straight stalks, with bands, it is sometimes mistaken for bamboo. Three of the hybrids in the Park, probably named in a moment of passion, are named *Big Wet Kiss*, *Hot Lips*, and *French Kiss*.

IXORA

Found all over the Cayman Islands, this Asian plant (*Ixora coccinea*) is also known as Flame of the Forest. It produces large showy clusters of flowers and in various varieties these can be either red, yellow, orange, pink, or white. Ixora is in bloom virtually every day of the year.

MEXICAN FLAME VINE

The arch connecting the "Red Garden" to the "Orange Garden" is covered with the Mexican Flame Vine (*Pseudogynoxys chenopodioides*). It is very fast growing and is actually a member of the Daisy family, as can be seen from the flowers.

TEDDY BEAR PALM

The crown shaft is that part of the leaf of the palm that wraps around the trunk. On this palm (*Dypsis lastelliana*), the crown shaft is orange and fuzzy. Somebody thought it looked like a teddy bear—hence the name. From Madagascar, it is also called Sira or Ravintsira meaning Salt or Salt Leaf owing to the former practice there of making salt from the pith.

SHRIMP PLANT

This plant (*Justicia brandegeana*) actually produces white flowers, but because of the extensive brown-orange bracts protecting the flowers, the plant in full bloom has a distinctive orange appearance. It is shaped somewhat like a shrimp.

TAYNA BRAENDLE SLATTERY

One of the Cayman Islands showiest native ornamentals is *Hamelia cuprea* shown here with its orange and yellow flowers in the Orange Garden.

Left: **A Fritillary Butterfly (*Agraulis vanillae*) obtaining nectar from the Mexican Flame Vine (*Pseudogynoxys chenopodioides*).**

TANJA BRAENDLE SLATTERY

MIGUEL ESCALANTE

DOUBLE POMEGRANATE

The double flowers, a feature of this plant (*Punica granatum flore-pleno*), mean that it is sterile and cannot produce the fruit from which it gains its name. Ornamentally, however, the flowers are much larger (four to five inches across) than in the fruit-bearing variety.

MIGUEL ESCALANTE

Top: Along the path through the Orange Garden with Canary Island Date Palms (*Phoenix canariensis*) in the background, the orange leaves of Bromeliad (*Aechmea blanchetiana*) in the foreground and Park gardeners planting out a new planting of annuals.

Left: Drought-tolerant *Lantana camara* provides year-round colour with its two-toned flowers.

The Blue Garden

This area encompasses three shades of colour (blue; purple; and lavender). It starts along the lake and follows the curving shape of the shoreline. A major feature of the garden is a long pergola painted blue. It is the largest area of the Floral Garden and is the most extensively planted.

VITEX

A shrub, found in the Queen Elizabeth II Botanic Park along the lake, Vitex (*Vitex agnus-castus*) produces long spikes of blue flowers several times a year. Because it attracts many butterflies during the day, it is often mistaken for a butterfly bush.

ANDREW GUTHRIE

Native to Madagascar, the majestic Bismarck Palm (*Bismarckia nobilis*) emerges above the Blue Garden.

Left: The inflorescence of the male Blue Latan Palm (*Latania loddigesii*) from the Mascarene Islands provide copious amounts of pollen and nectar for the local bees.

SEAN SLATTERY

TANJA BRAENDLE SLATTERY

Steeped in mystery and lore in its native South America, Thorn Apples are useful medicinal plants, but only by those who know how to use it as its toxins can be very lethal. Here the purple double flowered Thorn Apple (*Datura metal* cv. 'Cornucopia') is growing in the purple section.

***Right:* The pond of the Blue Garden contains a variety of blue and lavender flowered Water Lilies such as this cultivar of *Nymphaea*.**

BLUE LATAN PALM

From the island of Mauritius, the silvery blue leaves of the Latan Palm (*Latania loddigesii*) are large and very thick and was used as thatch for roofs. It is found in both male and female varieties, but is almost extinct in the wild.

LIGNUM VITAE

Widely found in the Caribbean region, this slow-growing tree produces a very hard wood used in furniture and construction. With its very dark glossy green leaves, blue flowers, and orange fruit with red seeds, the Lignum Vitae (*Guaiacum officinale*) can be a riot of colour.

SKY FLOWER

On the pergola in the blue garden is a very vigorous vine that produces long hanging flowers. Visitors enjoy walking under the plant and brushing against the flowers. A very fast-growing vine, the Sky Flower (*Thunbergia grandiflora*) is an ideal plant to cover something unsightly in a large garden.

BISMARCKIA

Unlike the common flat leaf formation of most palms, the Bismarckia's leaves are notable for their curving shape. Often becoming quite a large palm, the Bismarckia (*Bismarckia nobilis*) can become a spectacular sight with its silver-blue leaves displaying distinctive swirls. Native to Madagascar, its wood is used to make planks and partitions and its leaves for roofing and basketry.

SEAN SLATTERY

TANJA BRAENDLE SLATTERY

YESTERDAY, TODAY AND TOMORROW

Also known as Brunfelsia (*Brunfelsia magnifica*), this shrub blooms in winter with flowers that are bright blue when they open, fade to pale blue by the second day, and become white on the third day before falling off—hence the name.

HOLMSKIOLDIA

A very vibrant blue flower with lavender bracts (*Holmskioldia tettensis*) makes for a very attractive sight. Native to Asia, it is also known as the Chinese Hat Plant because it appears to have the shape of Oriental headgear.

WATER LILIES

In the pond in this area, there are several Water Lilies with blue blooms. Unlike the shy Red Water Lilies that close by lunchtime, the outgoing blue variety (*Nymphaea*) stays open all day.

Native to India and a member of the Milkweed family (*Asclepiadaceae*), the Crown Flower (*Calotropis gigantea*) produces these unusual flowers that are very attractive to butterflies and moths.

CLERODENDRUM

A huge shrub, the Clerodendrum (*Clerodendrum quadriloculare*) produces white flowers, but the leaves are greenish on top and purple underneath. The flowers, in clusters, can be almost twelve inches across.

MIGUEL ESCALANTE

The ubiquitous Bananaquit (*Coereba flaveola*) feeding from the showy inflorescence of the Chaste Tree (*Vitex agnus-castus*). Though native to southern Europe, the Chaste Tree is one of the only northern plants that grows well in Cayman's tropical climate.

The Yellow Garden

Because it is a wooded site, the Yellow Garden is in more shade where the yellow colours show up in contrast to the darker surroundings.

YLANG-YLANG

An oil produced by this tree (*Cananga odorata*) is one of the prime ingredients for Chanel No. 5 perfume. Most visitors smell the flowers of this plant before they see it. It is an extremely fragrant tree, particularly at night.

MIGUEL ESCALANTE

MIGUEL ESCALANTE

Cassava (*Manihot esculenta*) is a staple crop throughout the tropics where it is grown for its starchy root. The yellow variegated form (*Manihot esculenta* cv. 'Variegata') forms a beautiful foliage plant in the garden.

Left: **Evocative of the Far East, a small grove of the Golden Stemmed Bamboo (*Bambusa vulgaris* cv. 'Vittata') provides light shade and colour to the Yellow Garden.**

VARIEGATED CASSAVA

The root crop cassava (*Manihot esculenta*) is a staple in Caribbean cuisine. Most varieties have plain green leaves on long slender stalks and are not grown in the garden. This variety is an ornamental because of its green and yellow leaves, but iguanas and agoutis will dig up the plant to eat the roots.

PARROT'S BEAK

Growing over the arbor in the Yellow Garden, this vine (*Gmelina philippensis*) produces long pendulous bracts containing showy yellow flowers supposedly shaped like a parrot's beak. In full bloom, it is quite spectacular.

BAMBOO

Most bamboo plants are green, but this variety (*Bambusa vulgaris* 'vittata') sports yellow stalks with green stripes. Actually a grass,

When in bloom, the Ylang-Ylang (*Cananga odorata*) produces a wonderful perfumed fragrance which travels throughout the garden on gentle breezes. One whiff of this tree's scent and you will understand why the oil produced by this tree is a primary ingredient of Chanel No. 5 perfume.

MIGUEL ESCALANTE

MIGUEL ESCALANTE

With large leaves that resemble banana leaves and colourful showy inflorescences, Heliconia plants provide a tropical jungle look to the garden. Here (*Heliconia* cv. 'Golden Opel') basks in the filtered light of taller trees.

bamboo is a very fast-growing plant often gaining as much as twelve to eighteen inches in length in a day. Notions of ghosts are connected with the bamboo plant because of the creaking sound caused when winds rub the stalks against each other. On a dark night, the sound can be unsettling, especially for those who don't know it's simply bamboo dancing.

BUTTERCUP TREE

Native to Central America, this tree (*Cochlospermum vitifolium Plenum*) loses its leaves in the dry season and produces huge double

Covering a pergola in the Yellow Garden is an unusual vine known as the Parrot's Beak Vine (*Gmelina philippensis*). Native to India and the Philippines, this vine's inflorescence has reddish-brown bracts from which emerges yellow flowers that resemble in shape a parrot's beak.

yellow flowers in clusters hanging at the end of each branch. In flower, lasting about a month, it is a very unusual sight.

HELICONIA

The plant is named for Mount Helicon in Greece.

CROTON

Because it grows in almost every colour combination and requires very little care, Croton (*Codiaeum variegatum*) is one of the most widely-grown shrubs in the Caribbean. It can also be circumposed very easily.

The White Garden

We are once again in a very open sunny area. This part of the garden is elevated, winding its way up a rise to the gazebo. From the gazebo, there is a panoramic view of the entire Floral Garden including the lake.

AFRICAN OIL PALM

Economically, the African Oil Palm (*Elaeis guineensis*) is the second most important palm in the world after coconut (*Cocos nucifera*) because it is the primary source of palm oil. In its native habitat, it is also a source of wine, thatch, and building materials. It has been added to the White Garden for the visual effect of its height.

BOUGAINVILLEA

Native to Brazil, Bougainvillea (*Bougainvillea spectabilis*) is one of the most popular landscape plants in the tropics. All Bougainvilleas have white flowers; what appears to be different colours of flowers are actually the bracts of the plant. It blooms best in the dry season and is covered with thorns. The plant is named after the French explorer and naturalist, Louis Antoine de Bougainville (1729–1811).

BAMBOO

Unlike the common straight stalks, this variety of the Bamboo

(*Bambusa vulgaris cv. Wamin*) is notable for the bulging shape of the segments. It is included in the White Garden for its unusual shape and height.

STEPHANOTIS

This vine (*Stephanotis floribunda*) produces very fragrant white flowers, widely used in bridal bouquets especially in North America.

SANDPAPER VINE

Also known as Petrea (*Petrea volubilis albiflora*), this is a very fast-growing vine that produces clusters of white flowers that can be mistaken for wisteria. The leaves have a very rough sandpaper-like quality.

BUTTERFLY GINGER

Taking its name from the butterfly shape of the flower, the Butterfly Ginger (*Hedychium coronarium*) is extremely fragrant; you're likely to smell it well before you see it.

Native to the West Indies, Frangipani Trees are referred to as Wild Jasmine in the Cayman Islands. Losing their leaves in the dry season, these hardy trees produce large showy fragrant flowers. These trees are sometimes referred to as Graveyard Plants as they were often planted in graveyards which resulted in them not being popular for planting in the home garden. Here a Frangipani (*Plumeria rubra cultivar*) has white flowers with a yellow centre.

The Shell Ginger (*Alpinia zerumbet*) is a large herbaceous plant that produces clusters of waxy white flowers tinged in pink. Here the inflorescence is just beginning to unfurl.

Below: Though Bougainvillea is native to Brazil, it can be found growing in every tropical country on earth. Thriving on drought, these tough thorny plants provide a kaleidoscope of colour in the garden. All Bougainvillea plants have white flowers; it is the colourful bracts that protect the flowers that give the colour that everyone enjoys. Here *Bougainvillea glabra* cv. 'Singapore White' produces larger than normal sized white bracts.

TANJA BRAENDLE SLATTERY

TANJA BRAENDLE SLATTERY

One of Jamaica's most beautiful endemic plants is *Portlandia grandi-flora*. Known as **Bell Flower** in **Jamaica**, this plant grows on lime-stone rocks and cliffs in its natural habitat; however, it has adapted well to gardens in **Cayman**.

MIGUEL ESCALANTE

The Pink Garden

Visitors enter the Floral Garden through the Pink Garden, passing through two stone pillars with urns of pink flowers and a pergola covered with pink flowering vines. Plants with pink flowers or pink colouration in the leaves are found throughout this garden, and a pond with pink waterlilies can be found tucked away behind a bend in the path.

CARICATURE PLANT

The green and pink leaves of this plant (*Pseuderanthemum atropur-pureum* 'Variegatum') with a very random pattern, leads to it also being known as Match-Me-Not. It is a very colourful shrub.

ANDREW GUTHRIE

The Pineapple Plant (*Ananas como-sus*) produces a rosette of spiny green leaves that is eventually topped with the delicious Pineapple fruit. In the Pink Garden the pink variegated Pineapple *Ananas como-sus* cv. 'Variegatus' is displayed. While much more beautiful than the common Pineapple, the fruit produced is dry and inedible.

Right: Considered sacred by many Hawaiians, the Ti Plant (*Cordyline terminalis*) is grown for the colourful leaves it produces. In the Pink Garden *Cordyline terminalis* cv. 'Pink Diamond' produces a splash of colour in the light shade cast by palms overhead.

MIGUEL ESCALANTE

TANJA BRAENDLE SLATTERY

Angel's Trumpet (*Brugmansia x insignis* cv. 'Frosty Pink') produces large pendulous flowers. Brugmansia plants are loaded with the narcotic chemical scopolamine which is used in minute quantities in skin patches to control motion sickness, but can be fatal if ingested.

ANGEL'S TRUMPET

Very poisonous if ingested, Angel's Trumpet (*Brugmansia x insignis* 'Frosty Pink') produces hanging flowers eight to ten inches long. The name derives from the bell-shaped pink blooms.

CORDYLINE

Also known as Ti plants, Cordyline (*Cordyline terminalis*), like Croton, is grown for its large decorative leaves that come in many vivid colours. In South-Eastern Asia, the Polynesians saw the green Ti plants as a symbol of divine power and felt that wearing red Ti leaves made them invincible fighters.

The Heritage Garden

This part of the Botanic Park was intended to showcase the plants that played an important role in Cayman's history. The displays include *grounds*, or areas where root crops and vegetables would be cultivated, the economically important Silver Thatch Palm, and the Medicinal Garden with the types of plants Caymanians used to treat various ailments. In the heritage vein, an old Caymanian house, circa 1900, owned by Julius Rankine from East End, Grand Cayman, was brought to the Park and restored, and a sand garden was developed around the house showing the traditional ornamental plants of that setting. The display in the Park is larger than would normally be the case in order to show as many plants as possible.

Sand Yards

One of the most striking sights in the Cayman Islands is the spectacle of a sand yard, usually found surrounding a Caymanian cottage and featuring white sand, neatly tamped down, interspersed with

ANDREW GUTHRIE

MIGUEL ESCALANTE

Facing page: The focal point of the Heritage Garden is the turn-of-the-century Rankine House surrounded by a traditional sand yard. In the foreground are the showy flowers of the Crape Myrtle (*Lagerstroemia indica*) that is known as June Rose in the Cayman Islands.

Left: Able to withstand drought and seaside conditions, the Crinum Lily (*Crinum augustum*) was a popular sand yard plant due to its large white and pink flowers that are just beginning to unfurl in this photo.

Bordered by conch shells and Periwinkle (*Catharanthus roseus*), the path to the Rankine House is *paved* with bits of coral that washed on shore.

TANJA BRAENDLE SLATTERY

33

Right: The small tree known in Cayman as Lilac (*Melia azederach*) is one of those rare trees that have blue flowers.

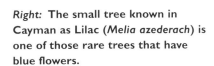

TANJA BRAENDLE SLATTERY

TANJA BRAENDLE SLATTERY

Left: One of Cayman's most beautiful flowering native trees is the Broadleaf tree (*Cordia sebestena*). This tree was often included in the sand yard garden due to its showy orange flowers. The rough leaves were once used to polish turtle shell.

various isolated plants. Adorned with conch shells and bordered by picket fences, the Caymanian sand yard has become one of the symbols of the landscape, and there was an earlier tradition of "backing sand" in baskets to add new white sand to brighten these areas at Christmas time. Some believe the sand yard idea was brought here by African slaves who would have been familiar with the practice in their homeland. Others contend it was initiated by the early British settlers since the white sand was reminiscent of the snow from their native country. Whatever the origin, sand yards can still be seen in the Cayman Islands. Of an evening, under a full moon, they make for an enthralling picture.

The old-fashioned roses were very popular in days gone by in Cayman. One of the most popular was _Rosa_ cv. 'Seven Sisters.'

TANJA BRAENDLE SLATTERY

TANJA BRAENDLE SLATTERY

Above: **Popular due to its drought tolerance and ability to grow near the sea, Allamanda (*Allamanda cathartica*) was found in almost all sand yards.**

The lacy leaf of the Asparagus fern (*Asparagus setaceus*) twines up the banister of the Rankine House in the Heritage Garden.

SEAN SLATTERY

SEAN SLATTERY

The curly vibrantly coloured leaves of *Acalypha wilkesiana* made it a popular ornamental in the old-time sand yard.

Below: Native to the West Indies but not the Cayman Islands, the Ground Orchid (*Bletia purpurea*) was introduced early to Cayman and quickly became a popular flower to grow in the sand yard where they would put up their spikes of flowers in March.

TANJA BRAENDLE SLATTERY

Grounds

The Cayman Islands were traditionally a subsistence fishing and farming community. A wide range of crops were grown in areas known as *grounds* which were usually cleared areas in the bush where pockets of soil were found. These grounds were sometimes at considerable distances from the residence as soil pockets can be few and far between in the islands and of small acreage. The favoured soil for planting an area of grounds was the red clayey soil known as red mole that is even less common than the regular type of soil found here.

Among the many crops cultivated were **Cassava** (*Manihot esculenta*) which grows into a large multi-stemmed shrub with attractive leaves. The edible portion of the plant is the thick starchy root that must be cooked prior to eating. The root can be utilized either cut up into pieces or grated, and a variety of dishes can be prepared including Cassava cake, dumplings, and bammy (a thin cake-like dish). Fried or boiled Cassava was also eaten with the meal, and was also a source of starch for the laundry. Tapioca is also produced from Cassava.

YAMS (*Dioscorea sp.*) were quite popular. Yams are vines that produce very ornamental, glossy, green heart-shaped leaves. The plant produces an edible tuber underground, and several varieties were grown in the Cayman Islands. The vines are generally trained to spread upward on a vertical pole for efficient land use. The tubers are baked to make cakes, boiled in the stew pot, used in soup, or fried.

OKRA (*Abelmoschus esculentus*), sometimes called ochro, is a member of the Hibiscus family growing into a large multi-stemmed, short-lived shrub. The leaves are rough and hairy while the yellow flowers look like small Hibiscus flowers. The flowers are followed by seed pods that are between five and eight inches long. These seed pods were cut up in soups (in the southern United States this is known as "gumbo") or steamed and eaten as a vegetable.

MIGUEL ESCALANTE

The primary source of sugar is Sugar Cane (*Saccharum officinarum*) which is a grass with a sweet-tasting pith. Children and adults alike enjoy cutting a cane and chewing on the pith to get that sweet sugar flavour. Rum is a by-product of the sugar industry.

One old-time crop rarely seen in Cayman these days is **WANGALA** that is better known elsewhere as **SESAME** (*Sesamum indicum*). This plant grows into a tall herbaceous plant that produces quantities of white one-inch flowers followed by small capsules that contain a multitude of seeds. The stems of the plants were cut when the capsules were almost ripe and were hung upside down in bags. The capsules would split open and the seeds would fall into the bags for collection. The seeds were parched and ground to be made into candy, and the parched and ground seeds were also mixed with ground hot pepper and salt and used as a meat-kind substitute when meat-kind was unavailable.

GONGO PEAS (*Cajanus cajan*), known as Pigeon Peas in the Eastern Caribbean, are still grown today. This member of the legume family grows into a large shrub that can be from three to ten feet tall.

Bananas and Plantains (*Musa* sp.) were an important part of the diet and their popularity remains today. Here green bananas can be seen hanging from the plant with the flower bud visible in the foreground.

MIGUEL ESCALANTE

The Queen Elizabeth II Botanic Park exhibits the essence of much that is best in the Cayman Islands. Here you will find beauty, peace and tranquility, together with the stimulation of the mind and imagination.

—Dr. George R. Proctor Botanist, expert on Caribbean flora, and author of the book "Flora of the Cayman Islands"

Right: **A** young **Pineapple** fruit (*Ananas comosus*) emerging from the plant's central rosette of leaves.

Below: **Related to the Hibiscus, Okra** (*Abelmoschus esculentus*) produces beautiful yellow flowers and the fruits are used as a vegetable in the Cayman Islands.

Facing page: **A** female **Papaya** tree (*Carica papaya*) heavily laden with immature fruit. The male **Papaya** tree is necessary for cross pollination, but never produces fruit.

SEAN SLATTERY

TANJA BRAENDLE SLATTERY

SEAN SLATTERY

Yellow pea-shaped flowers produce pods similar in appearance to green-pea pods, only smaller. The peas, either green or dried, were stewed with meat or cooked with rice.

COCO (*Colocasia esculenta*) is a very ornamental plant that is related to and resembles the large leaved Elephant Ear plant that is popular in tropical gardens and as a pot plant in North America. The starchy root was used in the same way as the yam. The root was used to make coco cake; it was boiled and served with the rest of the meal; and it was cut up and added to soup where it acted as a thickening agent.

While no relation to a northern Cherry, the West Indian Cherry, *Malpighia glabra*, produces copious amounts of bright red fruit with a slightly acidic flavour.

Other crops grown included corn, pumpkin, pineapple, plantain, banana, mutton pepper, sugar cane, and sweet potato.

MIGUEL ESCALANTE

TANJA BRAENDLE SLATTERY

Fruit Trees

Tree fruits were an important part of the diet in the Cayman Islands. A wide variety of fruits were grown and these fruits often evoke fond memories of childhood among the local residents. Some fruit trees would be planted close to the home, but often the trees would be planted in pockets of soil found scattered in the bush. The bush would be cleared around the soil pocket and the fruit trees planted. It is not uncommon to find an old Mango tree or Lime tree in the bush today that are long forgotten trees planted many years ago.

MANGO

The most popular of all fruit trees is the Mango tree (*Mangifera indica*). A native of India, the Mango is a large tree growing anywhere from thirty to one hundred feet with glossy dark green

The most famous and most economically important palm tree in the world is the Coconut (*Cocos nucifera*). Pictured are the fruits of the Coconut palm. Each fruit contains one large seed that is the brown "furry" Coconut that northern visitors are familiar with in their grocery stores.

TANJA BRAENDLE SLATTERY

The large starchy fruit of the Breadfruit tree (*Artocarpus altilis*). Once ripe, these fruits will need to be cooked before they can be eaten.

leaves. The delicious kidney-shaped fruits are produced during the summer months to the delight of residents and tourists alike. Many varieties of Mangoes are available today, but in the past only a few types could be found in Cayman. These early types included the Julie Mango that is still a favourite with many people, but some of the older varieties are difficult to find these days such as the Turpentine Mango, Peppermint Mango, and Number 11 Mango.

BREADFRUIT

Native to the south Pacific, Breadfruit (*Artocarpus altilis*) grows into a large tree with very large ornamental leaves that can range in length from nine inches to thirty-six inches long and are deeply lobed. The fruit is large, spherical, and can grow to eighteen inches in length and twelve inches in diameter with the colour being green to yellowish-green. The interior of the fruit is white or yellow and is starchy. This is a fruit that must be cooked prior to eating and there are many ways of preparing it. Common forms of preparation include baking, boiling, or roasting. The plants were brought to the Caribbean in the era of slavery to provide a cheap and plentiful food staple for the slaves.

COCONUT

Probably the one plant that most evokes the idea of a tropical island paradise is the Coconut tree (*Cocos nucifera*). This palm tree from the south Pacific is now found throughout the tropical world where it offers shade, coconuts, and a range of other useful products. Coconuts take about twelve months to develop from flower to mature fruit and one tree can produce between twelve and eighteen bunches of fruit per year. The single seed inside the Coconut fruit is the world's second largest seed and is very nutritious. The clear liquid found inside is called Coconut water and is a refreshing drink while the white endosperm that lines the inside walls of the seed is called Coconut meat or, in its early stages, jelly. The mature meat is usually chopped or grated and is use to produce a wide range of food items. Coconut milk is the white liquid produced when the mature meat is grated and squeezed dry.

SHADDOCK

The Shaddock (*Citrus maxima*) is an old-time fruit tree that is very difficult to find nowadays. Sometimes called Pummelo in other countries, this citrus tree is not only similar to a Grapefruit, it is one of the Grapefruit's parents. The Grapefruit (*Citrus x paradisi*) is a hybrid between the Shaddock and the Orange. The tree can grow from sixteen to fifty feet with a somewhat crooked trunk and looks like a typical citrus tree. The fairly large fruits have a very thick rind with a sweet juicy interior. The Shaddock tree was a very popular fruit tree until the Grapefruit was introduced. Other traditional citrus grown include the Seville Orange (*Citrus aurantium*) and Lime (*Citrus aurantifolia*).

SWEET SOP

A very sweet-tasting fruit is the Sweet Sop (*Annona squamosa*). It grows on a small tree reaching from ten to twenty feet in height, with dull green leaves that are aromatic when crushed. The compound fruit is nearly round and divided up into many segments with a black seed in each segment. The flesh is white and very sweet. Sweet Sops deteriorate very quickly after ripening and must be eaten very soon after harvest. Two other fruit trees related to the Sweet Sop were also grown in the Cayman Islands and these were the Sour Sop (*Annona muricata*) and Custard Apple (*Annona reticulata*).

Other traditional fruit trees include: Tamarind (*Tamarindus indica*); Rose Apple (*Syzgium jambos*); Genip (*Melicoccus bijugatus*); Guava (*Psidium guajava*); Egg Fruit (*Pouteria campechiana*); Star Apple (*Chrysophyllum cainito*); Cherry (*Malpighia glabra*); and the Pear Tree (*Persea americana*) that is also known as Avocado.

I have enjoyed the beauty and tranquility of the Queen Elizabeth II Botanic Park on numerous occasions since my first visit almost three years ago. It has since become a "must" on the itinerary of all my guests at Government House and all have been impressed and delighted at the variety of flora on display throughout the year. The Colour Garden remains a particular favourite.

—Peter Smith, Governor of the Cayman Islands 2002

Medicinal Plants

As is the case with most societies in the tropics, the therapeutic value of plants has long been part of life in the Cayman Islands. Some of these traditional remedies are now becoming well known in aspects of alternative medicine.

EUCALYPTUS (*Eucalyptus sp.*)—The eucalyptus leaves are used as an antiseptic balm. As a tea, it is said to lower blood sugar levels.

COCONUT (*Cocos nucifera*)—Water from the young (green) coconut is reportedly sterile and is useful in cases of dehydration and as a treatment for kidney infections. It is recommended in modern medicine for cases of diarrhea.

SOURSOP (*Annona muricata*)—A sour-sweet fruit, widely grown. Soursop drink supposedly helps cure hypertension.

TAMARIND (*Tamarindus indica*)—Measles sufferers were bathed in tamarind leaf tea to soothe the rash of the illness.

ALOE VERA—Now known to modern medicine, Aloe vera has traditionally been used in the Caribbean as a laxative and to treat cuts, bruises, and burns.

ANDREW GUTHRIE

Though native to the Mediterranean region Aloe (*Aloe vera*) has been grown for generations to treat burns, scrapes, and cuts. Today this plant can be found growing in the Medicinal Garden.

DANDELION (*Cassia occidentalis*)—The seeds are parched and boiled into a tea to help diabetes.

SWEET BASIL (*Ocimum basilicum*)—A tea of Sweet Basil settles an upset stomach and is good for calming the nerves.

ROSEMARY (*Croton linearis*)—The dried leaves were smoked as tobacco to relieve asthma.

CERASEE (*Momordica charantia*)—One of the many plants in the world with a folklore history as an insulin substitute, this plant is used for many ailments. The fruit, nearing maturity, is used to make a cough syrup. As a tea, it is used for diabetes.

SEAN SLATTERY

A native herbaceous plant, Vervine (*Stachytarpheta jamaicensis*) was used medicinally for fevers and as a poultice.

VERVINE (*Stachytarpheta jamaicensis*)—Also known as Worry Vine, this is a very cooling herb that is useful for fever. The mashed leaves are warmed and used as a poultice.

HEADACHE BUSH (*Capparis cynophallophora*)—The stem and leaves are boiled to make a tea for headache; crushed leaves for toothache.

DOGWOOD (*Piscidia piscipula*)—The bark, especially of the roots, is known for its narcotic and even poisonous effects.

POMEGRANATE (*Punica granatum*)—The rind of the fruit is boiled to make a gargle for treating sore throat. Concentrated pomegranate tea, though not pleasant to drink, is used in cases of severe diarrhea.

Growing naturally along Cayman's seaside, Wormwood (*Ambrosia hispida*) was used for sprained ankles.

BLACK SAGE (*Cordia globosa var. humilis*)—For a refreshing health bath. The hardy fibrous stalks are also used as a toothbrush substitute.

COCHINEAL (*Opuntia cochenillifer*)—A form of cactus, the inside pulp was used as a shampoo and hair conditioner, and to treat wounds.

PERIWINKLE (*Catharanthus roseus*)—Growing wild in the Caribbean it was traditionally used to treat diabetes and slow the growth of tumours. Recently it has been found to contain two cancer-fighting alkaloids, vincristine and vinblastine.

BIRCH (*Bursera simaruba*)—As a tea, it is used to cleanse the kidneys. Applied to wounds, the leaves are said to help stop bleeding.

AUNT ELIZA BUSH (*Tournefortia volubilis*)—Used as a tea to relieve labour or menstrual pains.

FEVER GRASS (*Cymbopogon citratus*)—A commonly used plant, in hot teas, for colds and chills. It promotes perspiration.

COW ITCH (*Mucuna pruriens*)—This is a vine with hairy pods that can cause severe itching. Scrapings from the pods, combined with a fruit, are given to children to treat worms. The hairs cause irritation of the intestine and the expulsion of any round worms present.

THOM THISTLE (*Argemone mexicana*)—A very common tropical weed, its caustic yellow sap is used for removing warts.

TEA BANKER (*Pectis caymanensis*)—Its fine green leaves and yellow flowers make an invigorating tea for influenza sufferers.

Native to Africa, the large bold leaves of the Castor Oil plant (*Ricinus communis*) can be seen in waste areas and road sides where it has become naturalized. The seeds are extremely poisonous and are the source of castor oil, a purgative or laxative.

ANDREW GUTHRIE

TANJA BRAENDLE SLATTERY

TANJA BRAENDLE SLATTERY

ANDREW GUTHRIE

Left: The path leading towards the Yellow Garden.

Facing page, top: The early morning sun is reflected off the red leaves of this red flowering Water Lily (*Nymphaea* cv).

Bottom: The fruit of the Annatto (*Bixa orellana*) provide colour for months in the garden. The seeds of this large shrub are used to produce a natural food colouring for butter, margarine, cheese, and chocolate.

Far left: The variegated form of Mauritius Hemp (*Furcraea foetida* var. *Medio picta*).

The Woodland Trail

QUEEN
ELIZABETH II
BOTANIC
PARK

Since most of the Islands' undisturbed forest is difficult to traverse, the Woodland Trail was built to allow Park patrons an opportunity to get inside the natural landscape. The trail is four-fifths of a mile long and can be comfortably walked. Care was spent mapping the site and the trail to ensure that it passes through unusual or significant habitats, such as that of a very rare native Cockspur tree (*Erythrina velutina*) or a stand of thatch palm. It goes through swampy areas, dry areas, and some with large areas of soil. The land encompassed by the Trail makes up approximately forty acres, and is estimated to contain more than fifty percent of the native flora of the Cayman Islands.

A common resident of the woodland is the endemic subspecies of the West Indian Woodpecker (*Melanerpes superciliaris caymanensis*). Here an adult emerges from its nest in a dead Wild Fig (*Ficus aurea*) tree.

SEAN SLATTERY

West Indian Mahogany (*Swietenia mahagoni*) is a common tree along the Woodland Trail. Grand Cayman's woodlands were once dominated by massive Mahogany trees, but sadly these giants were felled over the years for their valuable wood. While today's Mahogany trees will one day reach the proportions of those earlier trees if allowed to remain standing, it will not be in our lifetime. The leaves of the Mahogany tree pictured have turned golden brown prior to its annual leaf fall.

MIGUEL ESCALANTE

SEAN SLATTERY

Along the drier parts of the Wood-land Trail, succulent plants can be found interspersed in the bush. One of the most impressive native succu-lent plants is the Corato Plant (*Agave sobolifera*). These Agave plants grow for about thirty-five to forty years when they then grow a thirty-foot inflorescence containing millions of yellow flowers. After blooming and seed set, the entire plant dies.

KEVIN T. KARLSON

The Zenaida Dove (*Zenaida aurita*) is becoming quite rare in the Cayman Islands due to habitat disturbance, but this dove is a common sight in the Botanic Park where the woodland provides it shelter and sustenance.

FRED BURTON

This large bromeliad (*Hohenbergia caymanensis*) is a Grand Cayman endemic. Naturally it is only found in four small locations in the George Town area on prime real estate. The Botanic Park has been relocating this rare plant to the Woodland Preserve in an effort to save the species. Many of these plants can be easily seen along the Trail.

MIGUEL ESCALANTE

Much of the Botanic Park's woodland floods during the rainy season. Pictured is Logwood (*Haematoxylum campechianum*) along the trail during its annual flood stage. The reflections of the trees on the water makes this location a favorite with visitors during the rainy season.

SEAN SLATTERY

Here the epiphytic *Tillandsia utric-ulata* that grows in a rosette form, has found Logwood (*Haematoxylum campechianum*) to be the perfect host.

The Botanic Park has an opportunity to demonstrate what can be done with local plants as a showcase for beautiful, yet sustainable and environmentally sound, landscaping practices. The Park can and should lead by example.

—Frank Roulstone (orchid grower)

ANDREW GUTHRIE

Epiphytes are plants that grow on other plants without harming the host. Here in the Epiphyte Woodland section of the Trail, epiphytic orchids and bromeliads abound due to the humidity created by the seasonal floods.

Below: Pseudosphinx tetrio is a large caterpillar with a distinctive yellow and black body and a red head. A type of Hawk Moth, these caterpillars are commonly seen feeding on the Wild Jasmine Trees (*Plumeria obtusa*) and they can strip the tree bare of leaves in just a matter of days. The caterpillar's feeding does not cause any damage as the tree soon leafs out again.

TANJA BRAENDLE SLATTERY

TANJA BRAENDLE SLATTERY

Due to the seasonal flooding of the woodland and the small bodies of water in the Botanic Park, insects are very abundant. These insects provide plenty of food for dragonflies which are commonly seen flying about the Park. Here a colourful dragonfly rests on a bromeliad inflorescence.

Bull Thatch (*Thrinax radiata*) is one of the three palms native to the Cayman Islands, and Bull Thatch Bend along the Trail was so named because of the abundance of these plants in this location. Here some visitors enjoy these native palms shortly after the opening of the Park in 1994.

CAROL WINKER

VIN T. KARLSON

ANDREW GUTHRIE

Several species of cacti are native in the drier parts of Cayman. The largest species is *Cephalocereus swartzii* that can grow almost as tall as the surrounding trees. Pictured is the largest specimen of this species in the Botanic Park that is found in the Cactus Country section of the Trail.

Inset: A common denizen of the Woodland is Grand Cayman's endemic subspecies of the Cuban Bullfinch (*Melopyrrha nigra taylori*). Here an adult male is feeding on the fruits of the Logwood (*Haematoxylum campechianum*).

The Woodland Trail offers a relaxing respite from the hustle and bustle of George Town. In the background is one of the trail's thatched shelters with educational signage.

ANDREW GUTHRIE

In the land donated for the Botanic Park there was a natural wetland area, part of a Buttonwood (*Conocarpus erectus*) swamp. This was developed into a small lake to serve as a habitat for aquatic birds and for its scenic value adjoining the Floral Garden. The lake is about three acres in size, and, with no rivers in Cayman to replenish it, it varies in size from filling up in the rainy season to being almost dry at other times. As more and more wetlands are lost to development, the lake's importance as a wildlife refuge is growing. For animal lovers and bird watchers, it is a popular location for photographs.

The Lake

SEAN SLATTERY

Two rare West Indian Whistling Ducks (*Dendrocygna arborea*) waddle down to the Lake. Whistling Ducks are endangered throughout the West Indies, and the Park's Lake provides a safe habitat for a small population.

SEAN SLATTERY

**Early morning light casts shadows
along the Lake edge.**

I knew this area when it was just wilderness, and I
know some of the problems involved to make it the
place of beauty and relaxation it has become. It
shows what can be achieved by a few dedicated people.

—Hubert Bodden (developer)

KEVIN T. KARLSON

A Pied-Billed Grebe (*Podilymbus podiceps*) with adult breeding plumage swims in the Lake looking for its next meal.

Below: An adult Tricolored Heron (*Egretta tricolor*) stands motionless on a branch sticking out of the water waiting for a fish to swim within striking distance.

KEVIN T. KARLSON

KEVIN T. KARLSON

Migratory, the **Blue-Winged Teal** (*Anas discors*) can be found on the Lake in the winter. Feeding on insects and submerged water plants, the **Blue-Winged Teal** is usually found in pairs. The male is on the left and the female on the right.

Right: One of the most common inland aquatic birds in the Cayman Islands, the **Common Moorhen** (*Gallinula chloropus*) can always be found swimming on the Lake.

KEVIN T. KARLSON

One of the most brilliantly coloured birds in the Cayman Islands, the Purple Gallinule (*Porphyrula martinica*) can often be found in the marshy edges of the Lake.

KEVIN T. KARLSON

KEVIN T. KARLSON

KEVIN T. KARLSON

Top: **A**merican **C**oots (*Fulica americana*) are migratory birds which can be commonly found on the Lake in the winter season.

Left: A common bird with extremely long legs, the **Black-Necked Stilt** (*Himantopus mexicanus*) is often seen foraging at the Lake's edge.

Facing page: **The Green Heron** (*Butorides virescens*) is a solitary bird that can be found at the Lake's edge and among the stalks of the Lake's **Buttonwood** (*Conocarpus erectus*) roots in search for fish.

Park Features

THE CONSERVATION ROLE
BY FRED BURTON

The Botanic Park is one of the few places in Cayman where the native dry forest can be appreciated and viewed in comfort. Also, because the area is that of a low elevation landscape, subtle variations in topography and flooding patterns trigger dramatic changes in the flora. This makes the Park an almost ideal outdoor classroom that plays a valuable role in local environmental education.

The Park also functions as a modest protected area—all the forest enclosed by the Woodland Trail and south of the lake is protected to conserve the area's native flora and fauna. Extensive areas of natural forest are the key to conservation of so many of Cayman's native plants and animals, and the Park's contribution is reflected in the abundant wildlife to be seen on the trails and in the gardens. Birds such as the Caribbean Dove (*Leptotila jamaicensis*) and the Cuban Bullfinch (*Melopyrrha nigra*), or plants such as the tiny unique Caymanian orchids, are indications of the health of the forest.

Even in the more managed areas of the Park, conservation care threads through at many levels. Native trees provide shade in the colour gardens, and the Park's semi-artificial lake now provides habitat for the threatened West-Indian Whistling Duck (*Dendrocygna arborea*) and a range of other waterfowl. Cooperative arrangements with government departments responsible for vermin control keep the Park relatively clear of rats and wild cats, to the immense benefit of all native wildlife.

Even an unremarkable area of landscape plantings may turn out to have a conservation purpose: several highly endangered, uniquely Caymanian plants are planted and cared for in managed areas of the Park. Each is a scientifically documented collection held as security against the potential extinction of the plants in their natural range.

Fred Burton and friend. Fred Burton, former director of Scientific Programmes for the National Trust and manager of the Iguana Captive Breeding and Reintroduction Project, conducted many of the site surveys prior to the construction of the Botanic Park.

DAVE MARTINS

THE BLUE IGUANA

If you happen upon a Blue Iguana (*Cyclura nubila lewisi*) sunning itself on the trail as you stroll in the Park, stop and wonder. You are looking at an animal that was until recently almost extinct. As recently as the late 1980s, a specialist commissioned by the local government spent two weeks roaming Grand Cayman's east interior searching for wild iguanas. He saw only two and concluded that without urgent conservation measures the Cayman Islands (and the world) would lose this unique and spectacular animal forever.

Soon afterwards, the newly formed National Trust for the Cayman Islands rose to the challenge, and began a captive breeding programme that included research into the ecology of the tiny remnant wild population. The Trust now operates a highly successful captive breeding programme in the Botanic Park, and beginning in 1996 began releasing captive-bred two and three-year-olds on to the trails and by the lakeside. By 2000 the released iguanas had started breeding wild in the Park, and the population continues to increase. It is a heartening conservation success story, which has attracted international attention. In 2002, plans are afoot to virtually double the area in the Park being used for the Blue Iguana breeding programme.

Like many reptiles, the Blue Iguana can change colour. When the iguana is cool its skin is darkened to various

A head-on encounter with a male Cayman Blue Iguana (*Cyclura nubila lewisi*).

TANJA BRAENDLE SLATTERY

Primarily a vegetarian, the Cayman Blue Iguana (*Cyclura nubila lewisi*) forages on leaves, fruit, fleshy roots, seeds, and sometimes on the Botanic Park's flowers.

shades of grey. The darker the skin, the more efficiently it can soak up the sun's heat, and iguanas like to be very warm indeed. A four or five-foot male takes an hour or so of strategic sun-bathing to reach the desired temperature, and as he warms his skin takes on the denim blue that gives this iguana its name.

Blue Iguanas are generally peaceful animals, solitary vegetarians for most of the year. Things change in May when the males may fight viciously over potential mates, and in June when females defend their nesting territories. Eggs the sizes of hens' eggs, are laid in an underground chamber that the female seals up when she leaves. Hatchling iguanas, each about eight inches long, have to dig their own way out and fend for themselves in a dangerous world. But spared from the unnatural dangers of wild cats and habitat destruction, the Park's hatchlings stand a reasonable chance of surviving to adulthood, carrying with them the renewed hope of a secure future for this extraordinary and magnificent reptile.

SEAN SLATTERY

FRED BURTON

MICHAEL GORE

FRED BURTON

The blue colouration of a **Cayman Blue Iguana** (*Cyclura nubila lewisi*) contrasts well against the red soil of the **Heritage Garden**'s grounds.

Left: Due to the **National Trust**'s breeding and reintroduction programme, the **Cayman Blue Iguana** (*Cyclura nubila lewisi*) is now a common sight along the **Woodland Trail** and other parts of the **Botanic Park**.

Facing page: An adult male **Cayman Blue Iguana** (*Cyclura nubila lewisi*) raises his head out of the plants he is feeding on.

PARROTS

The iridescent colours and childlike playfulness of the parrots of the Caribbean have fascinated man since prehistoric times. So much so, indeed, that the demand for pet parrots since Europeans first discovered the West Indies has sadly extinguished half the parrot species originally living in the region. But the Cayman Islands were rarely visited, and remained uninhabited until about three hundred years ago. Our parrots lived on, winging through the centuries over our dry forests and mangroves, now to be celebrated as the Cayman Islands' National Bird.

There are about two thousand Grand Cayman Parrots (*Amazona leucocephala*) living mostly in the eastern half of the island and they often visit the Botanic Park to feed on berries and seeds of the native trees. The parrots pair for life and breed in tall old-growth forests of higher terrain and in tall Black Mangrove (*Avicennia germinans*) and Royal Palm (*Roystonea regia*) forests where they can find hollow trees large enough to nest in. The Park doesn't naturally include any of these habitats, though in time some of the Park's planted Royal Palms may grow large enough, before they die, to offer potential nest sites.

MICHAEL GORE

Sitting in a fruit tree, the Cayman Parrot (*Amazona leucocephala caymanensis*) surveys its surroundings.

The parrots are most conspicuous and noisy early in the morning and late in the afternoon. During the warmer hours when they are feeding, they are often perfectly camouflaged in the green leafy tree canopies, and may only give their presence away by soft contact calls between mates or by the sound of seed husks falling from the trees.

Facing page: **A favorite native food source, the Red Birch (*Bursera simaruba*) provides copious amounts of fruit for the Cayman Parrot. Red Birch is a good place to look for the parrots when the tree is in fruit.**

Inset: **The Cayman Parrot (*Amazona leucocephala caymanensis*) is a common sight in the Botanic Park.**

SEAN SLATTERY

SEAN SLATTERY

THE NURSERY

The Nursery serves the twin purposes of propagating and growing plants for the Park's gardens and Woodland Trail, as well as generating revenue from plant sales. The Park is always trying new plants to exhibit in the gardens for added interest, and the Nursery is where the plants are first grown to determine their suitability for growing in our soils and climate. Some plants are acquired as fully established plants while others arrive as seeds or cuttings.

For the more rare and hard to obtain plants, stock plants are maintained in the Nursery. These are plants that can be used to produce new plants should the ones in the gardens die. The Nursery also acts as a *hospital* for plants from the gardens. Sometimes plants in the garden start to decline and they must then be dug up and taken to the Nursery where they are nursed back to health and where the staff try to determine the cause for the decline.

MIGUEL ESCALANTE

Trevor Leslie, the Botanic Park's longest serving employee, is working with some of the many plants grown in the Nursery.

Facing page: The most majestic of Cayman's three native palms, the Cuban Royal Palm (*Roystonea regia*) makes an impressive display at the Botanic Park's entrance.

Water quality is very important to the successful cultivation of plants. The Nursery has a well that has good quality water during the rainy season, but it must be monitored closely. As the weather gets drier, the salt content of the water rises to the point where the plants can be damaged or killed. At this point, purchased water is delivered via tanker trucks.

For island residents, the Nursery is a source of plants that are often unobtainable at the local nurseries. A visit to the Nursery can also provide insight in plant culture and care and is as interesting as a visit to the gardens and the woodland areas.

ROYAL PALMS

The Caribbean to me was sea and sand and coconut trees. To come to Cayman and find a place like the Botanic Park is a bonus I never dreamed existed.

—Jerome Hardy
(New Jersey tourist)

SEAN SLATTERY

THE ORCHID SHOW

Concerned about the conservation of native orchids, the Cayman Islands Orchid Society was founded by residents who also cultivated imported orchids and who soon moved to the idea of a home-based orchid show. The event was originally put on in other locations, but is now held at the Park each year around Valentine's Day that coincides with the peak of the orchid blooming period here. The show is a result of many hours of work by Botanic Park staff along with the forty-plus members of the Orchid Society and it is designed with two aspects—an exhibition of locally grown orchids, and a plant sale of specially imported orchids most of which are in bloom. The majority of plants in the exhibit are grown by members of the society with many of them being very valuable. Some members contribute as many as sixty to seventy plants to the effort. The event has also become an occasion for educating gardeners on the techniques of growing orchids, and the Orchid Society works year round to secure and protect orchids that may otherwise be destroyed in various land-clearing projects.

This Phalaenopsis was just one of many types of orchids on exhibit at the Orchid Show.

The annual Orchid Show provides beautiful orchid exhibits and information on orchid culture to the islands' residents.

NOWHERE ELSE ON EARTH BY FRANK ROULSTONE

The Queen Elizabeth II Botanic Park is home to ten of the twenty-six orchid species recorded from the Cayman Islands, and four of these are found nowhere else on earth. Of these unique four, the most commonly seen by park visitors is Cayman's National Flower the Wild Banana Orchid (*Myrmecophila thomsoniana*) that is abundant in all natural areas. This large tree-growing orchid produces beautiful white and purple flowers on stalks measuring up to six feet long. Sometimes subtle variations of the colour give way to eye catching bright yellow flowers. These remarkable plants have been found nowhere else in the world so their abundance here should not be misconstrued as being common. Like all orchids, they are protected by local and international laws. Look for the Wild Banana in the trees along the nature trail where its green to yellow pseudobulbs resemble a ripening bunch of bananas.

The park is home to another of Cayman's rare local orchids (*Pleurothallis caymanensis*), a miniature orchid found only on Grand Cayman. Very few plants have been found within the borders of the Park and its small size makes it easily overlooked. Look for the Pleurothallis on small shrubs away from direct sunlight.

The Dollar Orchid (*Encyclia boothiana*) is quite common throughout the Botanic Park, and the small spotted yellow flowers emerge in November.

RICHARD GROUND

RICHARD GROUND

Rapidly disappearing due to habitat destruction, Grand Cayman's endemic Ghost Orchid (*Dendrophylax fawcettii*) has no leaves. This epiphytic plant consists of a mass of grayish-green roots from which beautiful flowers emerge. Though not found naturally in the Botanic Park, this orchid has been successfully introduced along the Woodland Trail.

Also in this singular category is the Ghost Orchid (*Dendrophylax fawcettii*) which was introduced into the Park through the Cayman Orchid Society and seems to be adjusting well to its adopted home. A native of only Grand Cayman, this rare orchid is devoid of leaves. Its creamy white flowers emerge from *nowhere* in May and June with a delightful fragrance that attracts moths to pollinate in the late evenings. Look for the flowers in the Buttonwood swamp area of the trail.

Another unique Grand Cayman orchid adapting to life in the Park is *Tolumnia caymanense* also found nowhere else in the world. Rescued from a subdivision clearing in 2001, this tiny orchid is easy to spot when in bloom because of its bright white and pink flowers. It has been placed in several drier areas of the Trail and should be visible throughout June and July.

Cayman's native Vanilla Orchid (*Vanilla claviculata*) is also now at home and can be seen near the Visitors' Centre. Unlike any other orchid species, Vanilla resembles a long fat vine as it climbs its way through trees and across the ground sporting clusters of green and purple flowers.

As you walk along the nature trail, be on the lookout for the Dollar Orchid (*Encyclia boothiana*). This small orchid has pseudo-bulbs that are round and flat and festooned with bright green leaves. The stems have numerous half-inch flowers of yellow mottled with little brown spots. A lover of humidity it is usually near to a water hole or swampy area. Once found throughout the tropics, this little orchid is becoming rarer as its habitat is destroyed for development.

Among the leaves along the Woodland Trail you will find the home of three ground-dwelling orchids. The most common and distinct of these is the naturalised *Oeceoclades maculata* with lovely mottled green leaves and small white and pink flowers. The flowers are self-pollinating and are thus short lived. With no natural enemies, it is quite common in drier areas of the nature trail. The same environment hosts *Cyclopogon elatus* and *Prescottia oligantha*. Both are very difficult to spot due to their small size and because of their habit of *hibernating* in the dry season. Their light green leaves can be seen from June to November, and the tiny flower stalks emerge from the ground for a few weeks in January and February.

Rarest of all orchids within the Park is *Cyrtopodium punctatum*, or Bee Swarm Orchid. In the development of the Park one plant was found and it remains the only example found to date here. This plant is now carefully protected and only a few people know its location. The Bee Swarm Orchid is named for the clusters of bright yellow and black flowers tightly packed to the branching stalk.

In addition to native orchids, the Park is home to many other orchids including some from neighboring islands and around the world. The trees around the Visitor's Centre abound with orchids, and there is also a growing collection of showy hybrid orchids that are displayed when in bloom.

The national flower of the Cayman Islands and the most well known of Cayman's twenty six native orchids is the Banana Orchid (*Myrmecophila thomsoniana*). This orchid blooms in June giving the Woodland a natural floral display.

CAROL WINKER

THE UNIQUE PISONIA

Pisonia margaretea—First discovered in 1994 a few miles from town, this scrubby tree is endemic to Spotts, Grand Cayman where a grand total of 23 trees are known to exist. Samples were sent to the Royal Botanic Gardens, Kew, in the United Kingdom and to the Missouri Botanical Gardens in the United States of America and both institutions declared the plant to be a an undescribed species. The

trees were found growing close to the main road and could have been lost to roadside clearing. In 1996, three residents (Fred Burton, Margaret Stelling, and Andrew Guthrie) collected cuttings from all twenty-three plants and took them to the Botanic Park Nursery where they rooted and were grown into sizable plants. In 2001 the plants were planted in various parts of the Woodland Preserve as part of a conservation project to save the species.

In order to conserve a species, a representative genetic sample must be saved. As with animals and people, each individual plant is genetically unique and to maintain genetic diversity and a healthy population, a large sample of the population must be conserved. The number of individuals that must be saved is based on the size of the population. As the Pisonia population only has twenty-three known members, we are able to conserve 100 percent.

This plant is a member of the *Nyctaginaceae* family that includes Bougainvillea though the Pisonia has no ornamental qualities.

What *Pisonia margaretea* lacks in beauty, it makes up for in rarity and uniqueness. This rare endemic tree, only discovered in 1994, occurs naturally in a small area of Spotts and nowhere else on earth. The Botanic Park has propagated these trees and established them in the Park where they will be protected should their natural habitat disappear.

MIGUEL ESCALANTE

USEFUL PLANTS

Traditionally Caymanians have found many of the native and introduced plants to be useful as building materials, sources of medicine and a host of other purposes. Some of the plants that were found to be of great value in the past include:

BULL RUSH (*Zamia integrifolia*)—A member of the ancient Cycad family, Bull Rush is often mistakenly thought to be a type of palm

MIGUEL ESCALANTE

The Cayman Rosemary (*Croton linearis*) is an attractive native plant found in rocky thickets. Rosemary has traditional medicinal uses and the dried stems were used to make the old-time Rosemary brooms.

because the leaves are similar in appearance. Bull Rush can be found growing in rocky woodland areas of all three islands and is scattered throughout the Botanic Park. Some plants are male and some are female, and the female plants produce *cones* that contain bright red fruits. The root, which is actually a subterranean trunk, is thick and

MIGUEL ESCALANTE

The large fruit of the Calabash or Gourd Tree (_Crescentia cujete_) remain green when ripe but cannot be eaten. The hard fruits are used to make bowls, dippers, water containers, and other utensils.

starchy. In days past this root would be dug up, grated, and boiled to make a porridge that was fed to babies and eaten by adults, too.

CALABASH or **GOURD** (_Crescentia cujete_)—Native to Florida, the West Indies and continental tropical America, the Gourd tree produces a fruit that cannot be eaten but was very useful to the early residents of these islands. The tree can grow up to ten meters but is usually smaller and is very coarse textured in appearance. The fruits are large with a very hard shell which are called Gourds or Calabash which is a corruption of the Spanish word _calabazo_ meaning "gourd." When ripe these large fruits were harvested, the smelly pulp inside was scraped out, and the shells were used as dippers, bowls, canteens for drinking water, and a host of other uses.

ROSEMARY (_Croton linearis_)—An aromatic shrub that grows one to two meters in rocky thickets and old pastures. The branches were cut from wild growing plants in the bush and tied together in bundles that were attached to a wooden handle to make the old-time Cayman Rosemary brooms used to sweep dwellings and yards.

COTTON (_Gossypium hirsutum_)—Most people are surprised to learn that Cotton is a member of the Hibiscus family; however, one look at the Hibiscus-like flower shows the family resemblance. Cotton is a coarse herb or shrub up to four meters tall and can be found growing on the edges of woodland and pastures where the dried fruit split open to reveal the pure white cotton fibers that surround the seeds. Cotton was collected in times past, and, to a small extent, exported.

BANANA and **PLANTAIN** (*Musa sp.*)—While the virtues of Banana and Plantain fruits are known to all, the leaves of these plants were also quite useful. The central rib or vein was removed from the dried leaves and they were then used to stuff mattresses which were called "trash plantain mattresses".

SEA GRAPE (*Coccoloba uvifera*)—The wood of this large seaside shrub or tree was the wood of choice when producing white lime (the daub) for the traditional wattle and daub houses that were once common in Grand Cayman. The green logs of the Sea Grape were cut and certain types of coral rocks were collected on the shore. The logs and the coral were placed in a lime kiln and they were burned down to produce the lime for making daub. Sea Grape is common along all of Cayman's coastline and can be found growing in the Heritage Garden.

A member of the Hibiscus family, wild Cotton (*Gossypium hirsutum var. punctatum*) produces fibers that are used to produce textiles. Cotton grow wild in the Cayman Islands where the dried fruits, or cotton bolls, were collected and used to fill pillows, cushions, and pin cushions.

SEAN SLATTERY

81

TANJA BRAENDLE SLATTERY

Cayman's only native Cycad (*Zamia integrifolia*) is referred to as Bullrush in Cayman. The large starchy root was once used to make porridge and baby food in the Cayman Islands.

DANGEROUS PLANTS

MANCHINEEL (*Hippomane mancinella*)—A member of the Euphorbia family which includes the ornamental Poinsettia, Manchineel is native to all three Cayman Islands plus most islands in the West Indies and tropical America where it is found on seasonally flooded land and sandy seashores. Its milky sap is a strong skin irritant, and one should never stand under a Manchineel tree during a rain as the oil from the leaves contains the irritant. The fruits look like small green apples and are highly toxic to humans though the Cayman Blue Iguana relishes eating them. The dried wood was used to make cabinets and as deck planking on wooden schooners. Manchineel trees can be found along the Woodland Trail where they are marked with red plant labels warning of their danger. If you are exposed to Manchineel, wash the affected skin immediately with soap and water as the active ingredient is water-soluble.

MAIDEN PLUM (*Comocladia dentata*)—A small tree or large shrub up to 6 meters in height, Maiden Plum is native to Grand Cayman. It is a hardy plant, thriving in dry pastures or even rock fissures, and when a piece of land is cleared it is one of the first plants to

This rather nondescript native shrub called **Lady Hair** (*Malpighia cubensis*) can cause misery for anyone who accidentally encounters it. The undersides of the leaves have small stinging or urticating hairs that can cause discomfort to skin that becomes exposed to it.

ANDREW GUTHRIE

Among the most dangerous plants in the Cayman Islands is Maiden Plum (*Comocladia dentata*) which is in the same family as the Mango and Cashew. The shiny leaves exude an oil that can cause extreme blistering and scars if touched.

re-colonize. The large shiny dark-green leaves can be easily recognized and avoided. The sap, once used for tattooing in Grand Cayman, is a very strong skin irritant and is highly corrosive. The active ingredient is not water-soluble and cannot be easily washed off after exposure. The itching and skin lesions can take up to two weeks to subside. In the Botanic Park, Maiden Plum is removed when found, however, one large specimen is maintained on the Woodland Trail with its leaves pruned out of reach as we believe the best way to avoid Maiden Plum is to learn what it looks like.

LADY HAIR (*Malpighia cubensis*)—Native to Grand Cayman and Cuba, this innocuous-looking plant offers a *surprise* to unwary hikers as the undersides of the leaves have stinging irritating hairs. The hairs have sharp points that easily pierce the skin, injecting a chemical that causes the skin to sting and itch for twenty or thirty minutes. One specimen has been left along the Woodland Trail to educate visitors of its dangers.

COW ITCH (*Mucuna pruriens*)—An herbaceous vine growing over shrubs and small trees, Cow Itch has a forbidding reputation in the Caribbean to the extent that construction workers have been known to boycott a site where the vine is seen. The stinging hairs of the seed pods can cause almost unbearable itching and burning of the skin and is very dangerous to the eyes. Due to its very dangerous properties, Cow Itch is not allowed to grow anywhere in the Botanic Park.

VINE PEAR (*Selenicereus grandiflorus*)—A member of the Cactus family, and native to Grand Cayman, Cuba, and Jamaica, the Vine Pear has trailing stems that climb high into trees in dense rocky woodlands. While not poisonous, the cactus spines on this plant have caused agony to many a hiker through the woodland. The plant is attractive because of its huge, fragrant, white flowers, but wrapped around tree trunks it poses a threat because of its profusion of spines. This plant is found throughout the Botanic Park.

Manchineel (*Hippomane mancinella*) is a very dangerous tree due to its extreme toxic nature. All parts are poisonous to humans, but the fruits are eaten by the Cayman Blue Iguana. This photo shows the trunk of a Manchineel tree along the Woodland Trail that has its dangers clearly marked. Epiphytes love to grow on Manchineel trees. Here the epiphytic Vine Pear cactus (*Selenicereus grandiflorus*) and *Tillandsia utriculata* find this Manchineel tree a good host.

FRED BURTON

USEFUL TREES

MAHOGANY (*Swietenia mahagoni*)—Originally much of the dry land in Grand Cayman was covered with Mahogany forest and records show the trees being cut from 1739 onwards to produce timber for export. The wood was used for shipbuilding, furniture, and coffins, and the bark was boiled to produce a dye for floors and cloth. Virtually all the old large trees are long gone; however, there are many young trees and the Botanic Park is home to many of them.

CANDLEWOOD (*Amyris elemifera*)—Found in rocky woodlands, it is rare to find large mature specimens. The wood is very resinous and will burn, even when green. In Cayman the branches (sometimes six feet long) would be cut and used as a torch as it would burn long enough to light up a hunt of lobsters at night. Stakes from Candlewood would be used as property boundary markers in Cayman Brac, and the flexible twigs were used to make wattles for wattle-and-daub houses. This tree can be found scattered throughout the Botanic Park.

IRONWOOD (*Chionanthus caymanensis*)—Ironwood is endemic or unique to the Cayman Islands where it can be found in rocky woodlands preferring to be near a fresh water table. The wood is extremely

Ironwood (*Chionanthus caymanensis*) is a large hardwood tree endemic to the Cayman Islands. So many of these trees were cut down for their dense termite resistant wood that they are now scarce. Those Ironwood trees that are growing in the Botanic Park, like the one pictured, are protected from future destruction.

hard, heavy, strong, and termite resistant so it was used in houses as foundation posts and as fence posts. While not common today, Ironwood can be found in undisturbed woodland such as the Botanic Park.

SMOKE WOOD (*Erythroxylum confusum & Erythroxylum areolatum*)—Two species of Smoke Wood grow in the Cayman Islands. The wood, which burns slowly producing a white smoke, was cut to burn in smoke pots to ward off mosquitoes. It was also used for fence posts. Smoke Wood can still be found today, but has been crowded out by the more aggressive Logwood plant that grows rapidly even in poor terrain.

Left: The Mahogany tree (*Swietenia mahagoni*) was once Cayman's most economically important hardwood tree due to the fine quality of its wood. Thousands of these trees were cut for shipbuilding, furniture-making and other uses that required fine wood. Mahogany is still plentiful today but only young trees can be found as the large old ones are all gone. Pictured is a Mahogany tree growing along the Woodland Trail. Bull Thatch palm (*Thrinax radiata*) is to the right.

The wood of the Smokewood tree (*Erythroxylum areolatum*) was burnt in smoke pots to ward off mosquitos in the days before mosquito controls. This specimen along the Woodland Trail shows the very rough bark that epiphytic plants find preferable as a place to grow.

THATCH PALM

An integral part of the history of the Cayman Islands is the story of the Silver Thatch Palm (*Coccothrinax proctorii*). Rope made from the dried leaves of the plant was a key ingredient in the Cayman economy of yesteryear, being used either for export or to barter for supplies. The dried leaves, torn into strips, was also the raw material for a variety of items (baskets, bags, hats, and mats), serving individual needs and for use in sales or bartering. The leaves of the palm, woven on slats, also served as very effective roofing, and this natural covering, with its distinctive geometric pattern, still finds occasional use today in the Cayman Islands, contrasting against the modern structures with a reminder of things past. The thatch palm is still found growing naturally in rocky areas all across the Islands and is widely present in the Botanic Park.

TANJA BRAENDLE SL*

SEAN SLATTERY

The Silver Thatch Palm (*Coccothrinax proctorii*) growing in the rocky environment of the Woodland Trail.

Above right: The traditional method of thatching roofs in the Cayman Islands resulted in a beautiful pattern on the underside. The shelters along the Woodland Trail exhibit this dying art. Pictured is the underside of a Woodland Trail shelter with a thatched roof made from the Silver Thatch Palm (*Coccothrinax proctorii*).

SEAN SLATTERY

A close-up of a leaf of Cayman's only endemic palm, the Silver Thatch Palm (*Coccothrinax proctorii*).

MANGO MORNINGS

Once a year, some thirteen or fourteen varieties of grafted mango plants are brought in for sale, and cultivation advice for the fruit is provided by a visiting expert from Fairchild Tropical Gardens in Florida. This very popular annual event also offers for sale such mango products as chutneys, salsa, salad dressing, cookies, and cakes.

TANJA BRAENDLE SLATTERY

TANJA BRAENDLE SLATTERY

The inflorescence of the Mango tree (*Mangifera indica*) is attractive and is a harbinger of the sweet fruit to come.

Left: A cluster of luscious Mangos (*Mangifera indica*) ripening in the warm Cayman sun.

DAVE MARTINS

Miss Corinne Conolly of Gun Bay has been greeting the Botanic Park's visitors as they arrive at the Ticket Booth since 1994.

Facing page: **The avenue of the native Royal Palms (*Roystonea regia*) at the Botanic Park entrance.**

THE VALUE OF THE PARK

"In these times of increased public awareness of the natural world and of concern for the future of the planet, botanical parks and gardens are being thrust into a much more important role in our society. Gardens no longer have the luxury of just being pretty places for Sunday strolls, but now are expected to be active in research, education and conservation, and even to influence public policy. Today's more sophisticated travelers, too, have high expectations of botanical gardens; sated with theme parks, glitzy nightlife and suntans, they look to gardens and arboreta to enlighten them about the natural history and wonders of the places they visit.

"Botanical gardens the world over are enthusiastically embracing these new obligations and taking a leadership role in preserving the Earth's remaining green spaces for future generations and in inspiring those generations to continue the mission.

"Gardens are now taking their place alongside museums, art galleries and symphony orchestras as valued cultural institutions worthy of public support."

—**Don Evans**
Director of Horticulture
Fairchild Tropical Gardens
Miami, Florida, USA

DAVE MARTINS

The Visitors' Centre

The Visitors' Centre.

VISITORS' CENTRE PHOTOS BY DAVE MARTINS

The Botanic Park's Staff

STAFF PHOTOS BY DAVE MARTINS

Below: **Botanic Park Staff.** (*Left to right*) **Earl Lewis, Kirk Marsh, Olsey Dixon, Ambrose Bucknall, Derron Donaldson, Trevor Leslie, and Milton Byfield.**

Above: **Botanic Park Staff.** (*Left to right*) **Lucy Ebanks, Corinne Conolly, and Vernicia Watler.**

Right: **Botanic Park Staff.** (*Left to right*) **Timothy Rivers, John Lawrus, James Miller, Andrew Guthrie, and Kevin Eden.** (*Missing from photo:* **Michael Letterlough.**)

Below, right: **Botanic Park Staff.** (*Left to right*) **Marline Chisholm, Marva Jackman, and Loma Whittaker.**

The Park's Master Plan

The Queen Elizabeth II Botanic Park site plan.

The Lake

Heritage Garden

Floral Garden

Visitors' Centre

MIGUEL ESCALANTE

S ometimes you have to sell conservation in a roundabout way. When a teacher takes a class to the Park, they walk on the trail, they hear the parrots, they see the iguanas and the local orchids, they go by the lake and see the Whistling Duck, the cultivated gardens, and while that's happening you're converting them to the value of conserving these things. If you just took them to wilderness, most of them would be bored or complaining in five minutes.

—Kirkland Nixon

TANJA BRAENDLE SLATTERY

The variegated leaves of this hybrid water lily (*Nymphaea cv.*) are as beautiful as the flowers.